Christmas Fun

Messner Holiday Library
Christmas Fun
by Judith Hoffman Corwin

Julian Messner New York

This book is dedicated to everyone who enjoys Christmas and its many delights, especially my son Oliver.

All rights reserved including the right of reproduction in whole or in part in any form. Published by Julian Messner, a Division of Simon & Schuster, Inc. Simon & Schuster Building, 1230 Avenue of the Americas, New York, New York 10020. JULIAN MESSNER and colophon are trademarks of Simon & Schuster, Inc. Manufactured in the United States of America

Fifth printing, 1986
Design by Judith Hoffman Corwin
Also available in Paperback Edition

Library of Congress Cataloging in Publication Data

Corwin, Judith Hoffman.
    Christmas fun.

    (The Messner holiday library)
    Includes index.
    Summary: Instructions for an Advent calendar, bird feeder, tree decorations, gifts, cards, things to eat, and other Christmas "fun."
    1. Christmas decorations — Juvenile literature.
2. Christmas cookery — Juvenile literature.
[1. Christmas decorations.   2. Handicraft]
I. Title.
TT900.C4C66   1982   745.594'1   82-60648
ISBN 0-671-45944-9

ISBN 0-671-49583-6 Pbk.

Contents

For You!

Marvelous colored lights, holly, mistletoe, and beautiful Christmas trees covered with bright decorations, silver icicles, gingerbread cookies, and candy canes. Getting ready for Christmas is exciting, almost as exciting as opening gifts on Christmas Day.

Christmas Fun will help you to enjoy Christmas in a special way. It is full of ideas for making Christmas cards, decorations, gift wrappings, presents, and good things to eat. Best of all you will be able to make everything yourself, using mostly things that can be found around the house. You will also learn why we do some of the things we do at Christmas.

When you are making the projects remember to follow the directions carefully, be patient, and most of all, enjoy yourself.

Before You Begin

Make your own pattern

Directions for several of the projects in this book include patterns so you can make an exact copy of what is shown. You don't want to cut up the book, so make your own patterns with tracing paper. Begin by placing a piece of tracing paper over the pattern to be transferred from the book. Now, using a pencil with soft lead, trace over the outline of what is in the book. When you have finished, cut out what you have drawn on the tracing paper. Now you will have your own pattern.

Using your pattern

To use your pattern, pin it, or hold it down carefully, on the paper or fabric you have chosen to work with. Draw around the edges of the pattern. Then lift up the tracing paper pattern and go on with the other instructions for your project.

Materials you will need

The basic materials you need are readily available from stationery stores and art supply shops: cardboard, oaktag, heavy white paper and colored paper. You may have bits of cloth and lace at home, and the fabric departments of stores have remnant tables with small pieces. For details or accents you'll need colored markers (waterproof), pencils, or watercolors. You will also need a sharp pair of scissors and a good brand of white glue.

Preparing a work area

Before beginning make sure that all your supplies are at hand and that everything is neat and clean. Cover your work surface with newspaper to protect it from glue. When working with glue always spread a thin, even coat. A thin coat sticks better and is less likely to cause the paper to buckle.

Most projects in **Christmas Fun** can be made quite easily. Some may prove more of a challenge—but you can do them all.

Have fun!

8

Hurry-Up Advent Calendar

It's hard to wait for Christmas to come. Advent—the word means "coming"—is the four weeks before Christmas. So help count the days and at the same time make a beautiful wall hanging. This Advent calendar can be used year after year.

MATERIALS:

1 yard muslin (or an old sheet)
½" diameter dowel, 18" long
1 package gold braid or rickrack
24 small safety pins
felt tip markers (especially green)
white glue
scraps of felt, lace, fabric
colored paper
beads, glitter, sequins

METHOD:

1.   Cut the muslin into a piece that measures 18" across and 30" long. This will be the background for your Advent calendar.

2.   The calendar is suspended from a dowel stick. To hold the dowel, first fold down the top edge of the material 2" all the way across. Press down firmly with your hand all along the edge. Decorate the edge with a row of gold braid or rickrack glued down. Slide the dowel under the fold and then glue down the decorated edge.

3.   Now divide the muslin into the top section where the Christmas tree will be and the bottom section for the calendar. The top section is marked off by drawing a line with a pencil 18" from where the muslin has been folded for the dowel.

4.   Checking the illustration, sketch in the outline of a Christmas tree, using a pencil. When you are satisfied with your sketch, re-trace your lines with a felt tip marker, and color the whole tree green.

5.   The calendar should be drawn in the bottom portion of the muslin. Check the illustration as you are working, sketching in first as with the tree. When you are satisfied go over the pencil lines with a felt tip marker.

6.   Each box on the calendar represents one day. Using a felt tip marker, number the days until Christmas in the upper right hand corner of each box as shown. The rest of the space in each box will be for a small ornament which will be pinned to that space.

7. There are 14 different designs for ornaments for you to make—an angel, teddy bear, candy cane, flower, bird, fish, rabbit, house, wreath, gingerbread man, holly, stocking, dog, and cat. If you make two ornaments from some of the designs you will have the 24 ornaments for your calendar and Christmas tree.

8. Start by making a pattern for each ornament, then use the pattern to cut out the ornament from the material you have chosen.

You can use felt, fabric, lace, or colored paper. Add the details, as shown, with felt tip markers, beads, yarn, and sequins.

9. Safety-pin each ornament to a separate box on the calendar and during December transfer each day's ornament from the calendar to the Christmas tree.

This is a good project to do with friends because everyone can join in.

11

The Nativity

Nativity scenes have always been popular as a way of telling the story of Jesus's birth. Few people could read in the Middle Ages, and the church service was in Latin, so Bible stories like the Nativity were told in plays, or with wax or carved figures. People once made the figures in Nativity scenes to look like themselves—they dressed the figures in the costumes of the day. Today we try to make a Nativity scene that looks as it must have really looked at the time of the first Christmas.

Stand-Up Nativity Scene

Create a delightful Nativity scene that is composed of stand-up figures that will fit under your Christmas tree or on a table top. Everyone can take turns arranging the figures the way they want, and even the littlest visitor can play with the figures without hurting them. The scene can be packed away and saved to be used again next Christmas.

MATERIALS:

medium weight cardboard
scissors, pencil
tracing paper
felt tip markers
colored paper
scraps of fabric
small pieces of tinfoil
cotton balls
glue

METHOD:

There are patterns for the Three Wise Men, a shepherd, Joseph, Mary, and the Christ Child in swaddling clothes—the wrappings once put on newborn babies. Patterns are also given for the animals necessary to complete the Nativity scene—a rooster, camel, donkey, and a sheep. More than one sheep should be made because the shepherd will need a small flock, at least three sheep.

1. To begin, trace and cut the patterns, and then place them on the cardboard.

2. Cut out the cardboard along the pattern lines.

3. Checking the illustration for each figure and animal, draw in the faces and other details on the cardboard shapes with a felt tip marker. Now add bits of cloth and colored paper, as suggested by the illustration, to give the figures some variety.

4. The crowns can be covered in tinfoil. Glue cotton onto the sheep for their coats. Glue fabric onto the figure of the Christ Child for swaddling clothes and onto the shepherd and the Wise Men for their robes. (Instead of using fabric you could paint the clothes onto the figures.)

5.   After each figure and animal is completed, make supports so that they can stand up. Patterns for these supports are given in three sizes: one for all the human figures, one for the camel and donkey, one for the sheep and rooster. Choose the right size stand and draw it on cardboard. Cut it out and then turn the figure face down. Center the support on the back of the figure and glue in place. Allow the support to dry for 10–15 minutes.

6.   The figures and animals can be arranged in many different ways—enjoy creating your own special scene!

17

Christmas Carols

A carol is a special Christmas song or hymn which is full of happiness. Singers of long ago, called "minstrels," sang to their masters. Today this tradition is carried on by groups of children and adults going through the neighborhood and singing or caroling from house to house, or apartment to apartment.

When we have a white Christmas there's nothing nicer than to see, or be part of, a group of carolers singing as the snow falls. Here's a chance to make your own snowflakes, as well as your own choir of carolers.

Carolers

You can make your Christmas choir as large as you like with these fun carolers.

MATERIALS:

tracing paper
pencil
white oaktag or paper
felt tip marker

glue or stapler
bit of lace, rickrack, or paper doily
sheet of music (if you can get one easily)

METHOD:

1. Two basic body patterns are shown, one for a boy and one for a girl. Trace the patterns and then transfer them onto white paper or oaktag. You can have the girl wearing jeans if you follow that part of the boy's pattern.

2. Cut the paper or oaktag along the pattern lines to make the caroler.

3. Draw in the details of the face, etc., with a felt tip marker. Then finish coloring.

4. Turn the caroler face down and bring the two ends together in the back. Paste or staple one end to the other.

5. If you have made a long skirt, glue rickrack, lace, or a strip from a paper doily along the bottom to make the skirt look festive.

6. You can make as many carolers as you want, and arrange them as you please. If you have an extra sheet of music that you don't need anymore, you can glue it to a piece of stiff paper and this can be the base for your choir.

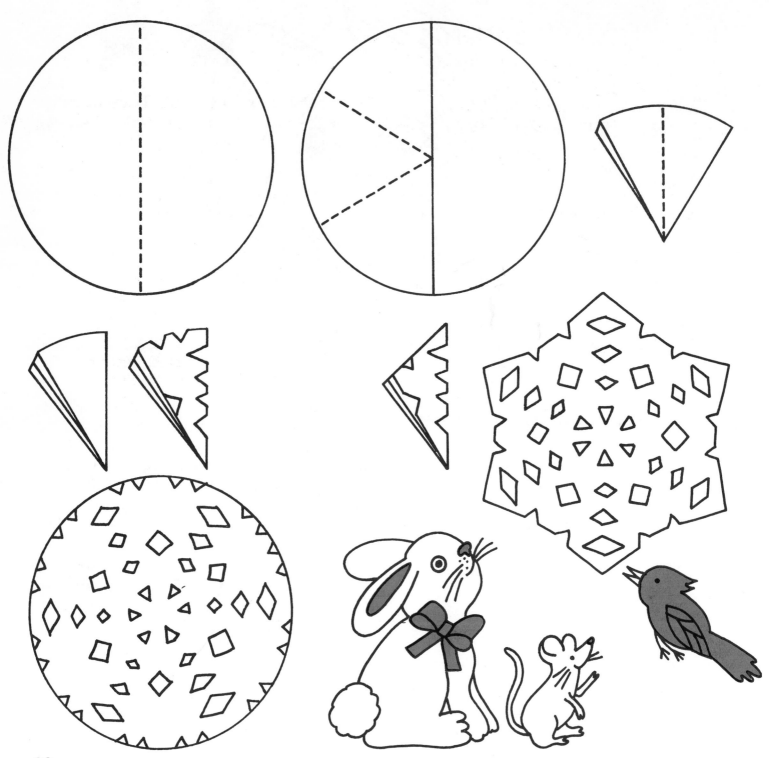

Silvery Snowy Snowflakes

Snowflakes fall gently to the ground and glisten and make us glad. They are fun and quite easy to make out of paper. You can make a circular or a six-sided snowflake, or both.

MATERIALS:

White paper or construction paper
scissors
glue, Q-tip
saucer
pencil
glitter

METHOD:

1.   An easy way to make a beautiful snowflake is to take a circular object like a saucer, and trace around it with a pencil on a piece of white paper. The bigger the circle, the bigger the snowflake you will end up with.

2.   Fold the circle in half, then in thirds, then in half again. Follow the illustrations as you go along.

3.   As shown, make small cuts along the edges, but be careful not to cut away any fold completely.

4.   Now open the snowflake and put a little glue around some of the edges with a Q-tip. Sprinkle glitter on the glued edge and when it is dry shake off the extra glitter.

5.   To make a six-sided snowflake follow the directions for steps 1–3. Then cut the top edge of the folded circle as the illustration shows. Be sure to make this cut on a slant.

To make your snowflake even fancier, make another cut on this edge as shown.

6.   If you start with a dinner plate for your circle, your snowflake will be large enough to write a message on. You could write "Merry Christmas" in different languages all over the snowflake. This would make a wonderful Christmas card. On page 59 you will find how to write "Merry Christmas" in many different languages.

7.   For a dramatic-looking snowflake, try cutting one out of tinfoil and then gluing the finished snowflake onto a piece of black paper. Glitter can also be used on this snowflake to make it extra special.

After you have mastered these snowflakes, experiment with your own way of cutting the paper to create your very own design.

Christmas Treats

When you think of Christmas what do you think of first—toys and other gifts? But what do you think of *second*? Is it a big Christmas dinner, a feast with all the "fixin's?" The idea of having a feast at Christmas dates back many hundreds of years. Each country has its own special food and treats for Christmas. But wherever the Christmas feast is served family and friends try to gather together to celebrate the holiday.

Here are recipes for making delicious Christmas treats so that your feast or other Christmas parties will be special. Christmas shortbread is a treat from long ago. The raisin clusters, cookies, and popcorn balls are right up-to-date. As for the bird feeder—human beings aren't the only ones who should feast at Christmas!

Bird Feeder

Share a winter feast with the feathered creatures in your backyard or neighborhood.

MATERIALS:

2 liter plastic soft drink container
2 feet of strong string
birdseed, pieces of bread or sunflower seeds
scissors

METHOD:

1. Empty and clean a 2 liter plastic soft drink container. Remove the label by soaking the bottle in warm water until the label floats off or can be peeled off easily.

2. Tie one end of the string around the neck of the container and make a knot.

3. About 3″ from the bottom of the container punch a hole with your scissors then cut an opening, using the hole as a starting point. The finished opening should be 3″ high by 5″ across. This will allow more than one bird to enter and feed at a time.

4. Fill the container with about 3″ of bird food.

5. Hang the bird feeder on a branch of a tree. Try to pick a tree that you can see from your window so that you can watch the birds feast and hear their songs.

25

Peanut Butter Chocolate Kiss Crunchy Cookies

A chocolate kiss candy is placed in the center of each of these cookies for an extra holiday treat.

INGREDIENTS YOU WILL NEED:

¾ cup butter (1½ sticks of butter), left to soften at room temperature for ½ hour.
¾ cup chunky peanut butter
1 egg
½ cup milk
3 cups flour
1 cup sugar
14 oz. package of chocolate kisses candies

UTENSILS YOU WILL NEED:

large mixing bowl
spatula
2 cookie sheets
Mixing spoon
Measuring cup

DIRECTIONS:

1.   Set oven at 350°. You may need an adult to help light the oven.

2.   Stir the butter and peanut butter together until well mixed.

3.   Add the sugar and the egg and mix.

4.   Add the flour and the milk. Mix well.

5.   Take a small amount of dough out of the mixing bowl and roll between your palms into a ball about the size of a big marble. Place the balls on the cookie sheet about 2″ apart. When all the dough is used up, take a chocolate kiss and push into the center of each cookie.

6.   Using an oven mitt or pot holder, place the cookie sheets in the oven for 10– 12 minutes. Makes four dozen cookies.

Christmas Shortbread

This wonderful cookie is easy to make. Only three ingredients are needed.

INGREDIENTS YOU WILL NEED:

1½ cups (3 sticks) sweet butter, left to soften at room temperature for at least ½ hour.
1 cup confectioner's sugar
2 cups sifted flour. Sift flour through a sifter or strainer before measuring.
Extra butter to grease the baking pan.

UTENSILS YOU WILL NEED:

13″ x 9″ baking pan
large mixing bowl
forks, knife, spatula
measuring cup

DIRECTIONS:

1. Turn on the oven to 350°. You may need an adult to help.

2. Grease the baking pan.

3. Thoroughly stir the butter and sugar together in the large mixing bowl. Continue stirring until the mixture is creamy.

4. Add the sifted flour and stir until well blended.

5. Spoon the mixture into the baking pan and then press it down with your hands, smoothing the top with a spatula.

6. Use a fork to make a pattern on the surface of the dough for decoration.

7. Divide the dough into 4″ x 1″ bars, using a knife to cut lines ⅛″ deep. (This is called "scoring".)

8. Bake 40–45 minutes or until very light gold in color. Remove from oven with oven mitt or two potholders. Cool in the pan.

9. Cut into bars along the scored lines.

Chocolate-covered Raisin Clusters

These candies are the size of half dollars and are easy to make.

INGREDIENTS YOU WILL NEED:

6 oz. semi-sweet chocolate pieces (chocolate chips)
2 cups raisins (or walnuts, or peanuts)

UTENSILS YOU WILL NEED:

medium size saucepan
teaspoon
measuring cup
large serving plate
tinfoil

DIRECTIONS:

1.   Put the chocolate pieces into the saucepan over a *very* low flame. You may need an adult to help. Melt the chocolate.

2. . After the chocolate is melted, remove from heat, add raisins and stir until thoroughly mixed. (Or use walnuts or peanuts.)

3.   Spoon the chocolate mixture by the teaspoonful onto the tinfoil. Place in refrigerator until hard, at least one hour.

4.   Store the candy in a jar. You may want to make a festive decoration for the jar.

Christmas Popcorn Balls

Sixteen popcorn balls that are easy to make and can even be tied onto the Christmas tree and eaten after Christmas.

INGREDIENTS YOU WILL NEED:

4 quarts of popcorn, already popped
2 cups sugar
⅔ cup light corn syrup
½ stick butter
1 teaspoon ground cinnamon
½ teaspoon salt
1 teaspoon vanilla
1 glass very cold water

UTENSILS YOU WILL NEED:

measuring spoons and cup
medium size saucepan
large mixing bowl
mixing spoon
plastic wrap

DIRECTIONS:

1. Mix together 2 cups sugar, ⅔ cup light corn syrup, ⅔ cup water, ½ stick butter, 1 teaspoon ground cinnamon, and ½ teaspoon salt in medium size saucepan. You may need an adult to help with the stove. Stirring constantly, cook over moderate heat until the mixture boils. Lower the heat and stop stirring. Continue cooking for a few minutes more. Drop a very small amount into *very* cold water. If the mixture forms hard threads, it is done. If not, cook a minute or two more and test again.

2. When threads form, remove saucepan from heat, add one teaspoon vanilla, and gently stir.

3. Pour this hot mixture over the popcorn, and stir with a spoon. Form into balls when cool enough to handle. Wrap in plastic wrap.

4. If you wish, decorate by tying ribbons around the plastic or pasting on tags.

Christmas Tree Decorations

The Christmas tree is one of the favorite symbols of Christmas. Usually an evergreen, the Christmas tree has its origins in Europe, long ago. Even before people celebrated Christmas, ancient peoples decorated trees with fruits and candles to celebrate the winter season.

The first Christmas trees as we know them were in Germany. They were lit by candles and decorated with gingerbread, cookies, nuts, fruits, and paper flowers. Bright-colored glass balls were invented later. Tiny golden bells on a tree were once thought to chase away evil spirits. The tinsel on the Christmas tree, legend has it, came about because once there was a very poor woman who had nothing to put under her Christmas tree for her children. But on Christmas morning the branches of the tree were covered with spider webs that had been turned into silver by the rising sun.

The Christmas ornament you make yourself is very special. Here are some ideas for your own ornaments. The Christmas dove is a symbol of peace, something we wish for always but especially at Christmas—the season of peace. The winged angel, and the snowman, are happy symbols of this time of year.

My "Me" Christmas Ornament

Create your very own personalized Christmas tree ornament. You can paint these stuffed ornaments with the colors of your favorite T-shirt or your school colors. You can even write your name on the T-shirt and give it to someone as a Christmas remembrance.

MATERIALS:

½ yard unbleached muslin
polyester batting
several small brushes
several colors of acrylic paint

straight pins, needle and thread
scissors
pencil

METHOD:

1. Make a pattern for the boy or girl ornament by tracing the design given.

2. Take the muslin and fold it in half. Pin the muslin so it holds together and you can cut two at a time. Place the pattern on top of the muslin and trace around the outline of it with a pencil. About ¼″ away from the pattern line cut out the pattern, leaving the pins in. Remove the pattern.

3. Sew the two sides together on the pattern line, leaving a 1½″ opening for the stuffing to go through.

4. Clip the curves so that the ornament won't pucker.

5. Turn the ornament inside out so the rough edges are hidden, stuff, and then stitch up the opening.

6. Paint on the face and clothes that you like so that it looks like you. Or you could surprise a friend by making an ornament that looks like him or her. When it's dry, sew a bright thread through the top for hanging on the Christmas tree.

31

33

Winged Angel

Hang this on a Christmas tree, display it on a mantle, put several in a pretty basket of candy or fruit, or scent with perfume and give them as gifts.

MATERIALS:

½ yard unbleached muslin (this should make at least 4 angels)
polyester batting
white sewing thread
straight pins
needle, thread
scissors
pencil, felt tip marker
crayons
waxed paper, iron

METHOD:

1. Make a pattern for the angel by tracing the design given.

2. Fold the muslin in half. Place the pattern on top of the muslin and trace around the outline of it with a pencil. Remove the pattern and pin the folded piece of cloth together so it holds steady. About ¼″ away from the pattern line, cut out the pattern, leaving the pins in.

3. Checking the illustration, draw the details of the angel on the muslin with a pencil. When you are satisfied with what you have drawn, draw over the pencil line with a felt tip marker.

4. Color the angel with crayons. The back of the angel can either be crayoned in one color or the design can be copied as given.

5. Unfold the angel and place crayoned side up on an ironing board. Put a piece of waxed paper on top and gently iron to set the color and make it shiny. You will need an adult to help you with this.

6. With the sides that have been colored facing each other, pin the angel together.

7. Sew the two sides together on the pattern line, leaving the pins in. Leave a 1½″ opening for the stuffing to go through.

8. Clip the curves with your scissors. This keeps the curves from puckering after the angel has been stuffed.

9. Turn the angel inside out and stuff. If the angel is to be scented, insert a ball of cotton that has been soaked in some perfume into the center. Stitch up the opening.

10. Sew a bright thread through the top for hanging on the Christmas tree.

It would be fun to make several of the angels wearing different-colored dresses and with different-colored hair. This project could also be a popular one to make and sell at school to raise money for a party.

Christmas Dove

This special Christmas dove is shown in two versions—a miniature dove that is perfect for the Christmas tree, and a larger version that is meant to hang in the window. The dove can be simple and white or decorated with fancy designs. You could even make a dozen of them and put them in your classroom window.

MATERIALS:

Stiff white paper or oaktag
Scissors
Needle
Thread or yarn
Felt tip markers

METHOD:

1. Trace the pattern on the stiff paper or oaktag.

2. Cut out the pattern. Checking the illustration, cut the slit in the body. The wing will go through this slit.

3. Using a needle, make a hole in the dove, as shown in the illustration, so that string can be run through to hang it up.

4. If you choose to decorate the dove, do so now before the wings go on.

5. Fold wing as shown along the dotted lines. Through the slit in the body insert the wing.

6. Run a piece of yarn (or thread for the smaller dove) through the hole and make a knot to secure the thread. The dove is now ready for display.

38

Christmas "Clay" Decorations

You can make all sorts of great things to decorate your Christmas tree with this flour clay. Patterns are given for a sun, snowman, rocking horse, doll, reindeer, and elf—all of which can be made out of one recipe.

An adult should be around to supervise this project.

INGREDIENTS:

2 cups flour
1 cup salt
1 cup water

UTENSILS YOU WILL NEED:

measuring cup
large bowl
cookie sheet

MATERIALS:

tracing paper
cardboard
pencil, scissors
acrylic paints
shellac, brushes
toothpick
colored thread or ribbon
knife

METHOD:

1.   Mix the flour and salt together in a large bowl. Then add the water a little at a time, mixing it in. When all the water is used up, mix the dough well with your hands. This is called "kneading".

2.   Continue to knead the dough until it is smooth.

3.   Put some flour on a clean working surface and then roll the dough to about ¼" thick. (The dough will expand slightly when it is baked.)

4.   Trace the pattern of the ornament you want from the book and transfer it to the cardboard.

5.   Place the cardboard cutout on the dough. Hold the cardboard down with one hand and then use your knife carefully to cut the dough around the pattern.

6.   Roll small pieces of dough for eyes, cheeks, and other features. Put some dough through a sieve (strainer) to make hair. Moisten the ornament with a drop of water, then put on the dough decorations. Moistening makes them stick better.

7.   With a toothpick make a hole at the top of the ornament so you can hang it up later on.

8.   Set the oven at 325°. An adult should help you. Place the ornaments on a cookie sheet at least 1" apart and bake until lightly browned. It takes about 30−40 minutes, but keep checking the oven to make sure that the ornaments aren't burning along the edges.

9. Using a potholder to protect your hand, remove the cookie sheet from the oven. When the ornaments are cool, take them off the cookie sheet.

10. Decorate your ornaments with acrylic paints. See patterns.

11. When the ornaments are dry, cover them completely with shellac to keep out any moisture and to preserve them. The ornaments can be used year after year and will become a permanent part of your Christmas.

41

Gifts

Long before there was a Christmas, it was a popular custom to give presents at festival times. The wealthy Romans would give the common citizens gifts, and in return they would receive wreaths of shiny leaves and incense. The children were remembered with small clay statues.

The gift for Christmas is a symbol of the gifts that the three Wise Men took to Bethlehem. They brought treasures to the Christ Child—gifts of gold, frankincense, and myrrh.

The Christmas stocking has long been a favorite part of Christmas. For more than one hundred years, children have hung up their stockings at the fireplace the night before Christmas so that Santa could slide down the chimney and fill them with Christmas goodies. In Holland children put out wooden shoes to be filled. In olden days a bad child would find coal in the shoe on Christmas morning! Today many of us no longer have fireplaces, but we still love Christmas stockings filled with gifts. The Christmas stocking is fun to make. The Christmas sneaker is for those of us who like something a little different.

Santa Claus Christmas Stocking

This can be hung up (to be filled by Santa himself?) or it can be a wrapping for a very special present.

MATERIALS:

1 squares of red felt
2 squares of green felt
1 square of white felt
1 square of black felt

scraps of felt in different colors or other fabrics
glue, scissors
tracing paper, pencil

METHOD:

1. First make a pattern of the parts for the Santa figure. Pin the pattern for Santa's face and beard on the white felt and cut out. Pin tracing paper patterns for the coat, hat and two mittens to red felt and cut out. Cut boots, belt, and mustache from black felt. Then place Santa on a green square and begin gluing him down. Check the illustration for placement as you glue Santa onto the square. Start with the face, hat, and body. Next add the beard to the face and the belt to the coat. Now the mittens, beard, and mustache.

2. To complete Santa's face cut out two small circles of black felt for the eyes, and a larger circle of red felt for the nose. Lastly, cut out the heart shape from the white felt or a gay piece of fabric and glue in place.

3. Draw a stocking outline around your Santa. (For the shape, see drawing.)

4. Pin the stocking pattern on another piece of green felt. This will be the back of the stocking.

5. Now put both sides of the stocking together with the Santa side on top. Glue all along the outside edges.

6. To hang your stocking, cut a 6″ by 1″ strip of green felt. Fold the strip in half and glue in place, as shown.

43

44

Christmas Sneaker

You can fill this funny sneaker with Christmas goodies or give it to a friend as a gift.

MATERIALS:
2 squares of red felt (standard 4″ size)⎱ or use felt the colors
1 square of green felt ⎰ of your sneakers
1 white shoelace
glue, tracing paper
pencil
scissors

METHOD:

1. Make a tracing of the pattern for the sneaker itself, the stripes, and the star designs.

2. Cut out the stars and stripes, using green felt, or the color of your choice.

3. Put the two red (or your color) squares on top of each other and then pin the sneaker pattern on top of them. Cut out.

4. Check the illustration for placement as you glue the stars and stripes onto the sneaker.

5. Take the shoelace and glue it in place. Tie a bow at the ends.

6. Put both sides of the sneaker together, with the decorated side on top. Glue all along the outside edges, except, of course, across the top of the sneaker—that's where the goodies go.

7. To hang your sneaker, cut a 6″ x 1″ strip of green felt. Fold the strip in half and glue in place, as shown.

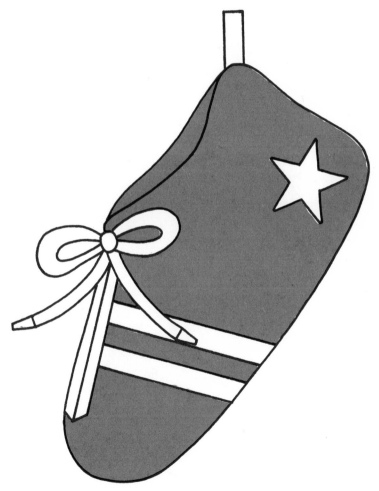

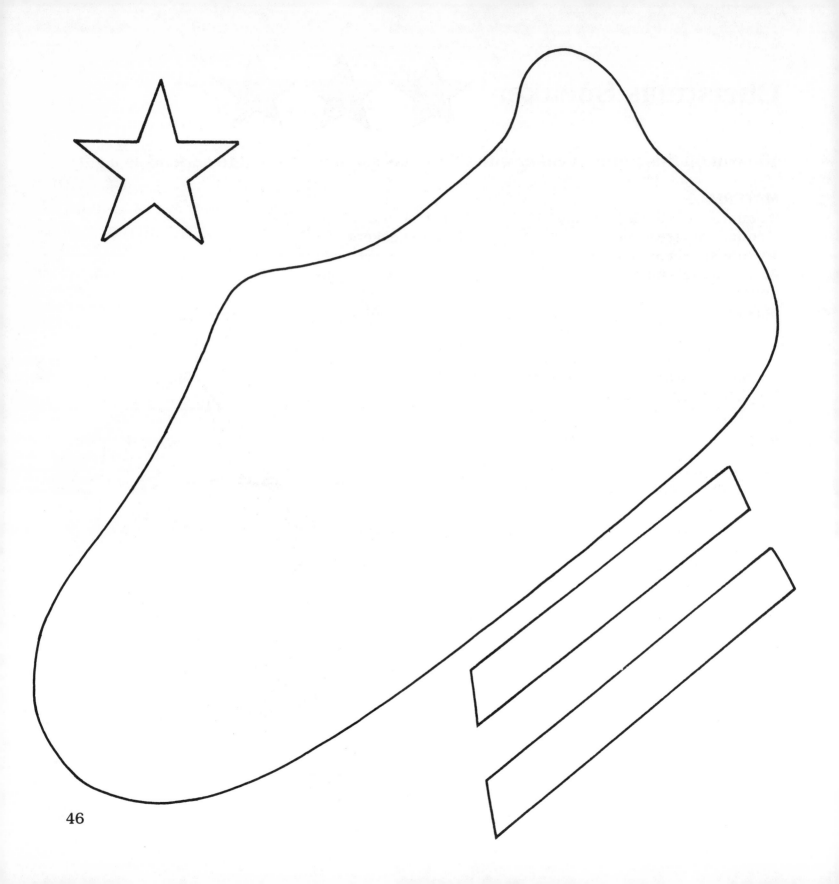

46

Evergreens

For hundreds of years before the first Christmas, wreaths of holly, mistletoe, and pine played a special part in winter festivals. These evergreens were used to decorate homes and shrines because they were beautiful and the green showed that they were living when all other plants seemed to be dead. People put evergreens on their doors for the woodland spirits to live in, warm and safe. The woodland spirits would in return bring good luck and good health to the family that gave them shelter.

The Christmas wreath we have chosen is not evergreen, but it's lots of fun to make.

Doggy Biscuit Wreath

MATERIALS:

Box of dog biscuits
Piece of cardboard about 12″ square
½ cup flour   ¼ cup water

spoon, bowl
pencil, scissors
12″ length of red ribbon

METHOD:

1.   Take a large dinner plate and place it on a piece of cardboard. Trace around the outside edge with a pencil.

2.   Now take a smaller plate, such as a saucer, and put that in the middle of the circle. Trace around the small plate.

3.   Cut out the inside circle, then cut around the outer edge of the large circle. You now have a cardboard wreath ready for decorating with dog biscuits.

4.   To make the paste that will hold the dog biscuits onto the wreath, mix together ½ cup flour with ¼ cup water.

5.   Put a little of this paste onto the back of a dog biscuit and then stick the biscuit onto the cardboard wreath. Continue until the wreath is covered with dog biscuits.

6.   Tie a red ribbon to the wreath.

A Christmas Play with Music

The Nutcracker is an enchanting ballet that is danced during the Christmas season. The ballet has beautiful scenery, especially a giant Christmas tree that appears in the first act, and the Kingdom of the Sugar Plum Fairy. Here is the story of *The Nutcracker* and some of the highlights from the ballet.

The music is an important part of the magic of this play. If you can, get a record of *The Nutcracker* by Peter Ilyich Tchaikovsky, the Russian composer, to use with your play—and to enjoy as you make your theater.

The Nutcracker

ACT I

It is Christmas Eve in a German village "in fantastic times." A man and his wife, accompanied by their guests, are placing the finishing touches on their Christmas tree. In a corner of the room there is a beautiful grandfather clock with an owl on top of it. Nine o'clock strikes, and with each stroke of the clock the owl flaps its wings. Now the Christmas tree is lit and the children are called into the room to open up their presents.

Drosselmeyer, an elegant—and mysterious—old gentleman arrives with a fantastic gift for Clara. It's a brightly painted nutcracker in the shape of a soldier. It is given to Clara, who loves it. Another child, Fritz, grabs the Nutcracker away from Clara and forces an enormous nut into the soldier's mouth, breaking its teeth. Clara is heartbroken. She picks up the toy and carefully tucks it into her doll's bed.

The children go off to bed, but Clara can't sleep because she keeps thinking of her precious Nutcracker. She goes back into the room with the Christmas tree and the grandfather clock. Now only the moonlight is shining into the room. The clock strikes midnight as Clara enters—but it is Drosselmeyer beating the time, not the owl.

Clara hears strange sounds in the distance. It is the sound of scratching mice! The Mouse King is leading the mice in a battle with an army of toy soldiers. The Nutcracker is leader of the soldiers, but they are about to be defeated by the mice. Clara throws her slipper at the Mouse King and then faints. When she awakes, the Nutcracker has changed into a handsome prince, and the mice have scattered. The prince thanks Clara for saving his life and invites her to go with him to the Kingdom of Sweets, where the Sugar Plum Fairy is queen. Clara and the prince walk off into the forest with snow falling gently to the ground.

ACT II

Clara and the prince have reached the Palace of Sweets. The prince tells the Sugar Plum Fairy and the court how Clara saved his life. They all do special dances to honor Clara. The prince dances, and so does the Sugar Plum Fairy. Then, as the entire candy court dances, Clara becomes a princess of the Kingdom of Sweets.

  The End

MATERIALS:

a carton from the grocery store
cardboard for the cutout characters, and scenery
fabric for the curtain, string
strong, all-purpose tape, poster paints
scraps of colored paper or felt for the scenery
felt tip markers
strips of balsa wood: ½" × ½" × the length of the stage
(at least 15 — these will hold your figures and pieces of scenery).

METHOD:

A.   The characters and scenery

1.   There are patterns for Clara, Fritz, Drosselmeyer, the Nutcracker, the Mouse King, the Prince, a mouse, a soldier, the Sugar Plum Fairy, and candy flowers. You will need to make several soldiers, mice and candy flowers for your cast.

2.   There is scenery for both acts: first a scene with a Christmas tree and the grandfather clock, and then a scene in the Sugar Plum kingdom with flowers.

3.   To make the characters and the scenery, first draw the pattern given on tracing paper; then cut the patterns out. Place the patterns on cardboard, and trace around the outline with a pencil.

4.   Checking the illustration for each character and piece of scenery, draw in the details with a pencil. When you are satisfied with your drawings, go over the pencil lines with a felt tip marker.

5.   Color the figures and pieces of scenery with felt tip markers. You can also add special touches with bits of cloth and/or colored paper.

6.   Glue the finished characters and pieces of scenery onto strips of wood as shown.

B.   The stage

1.   Seal the box flaps with tape. Cut a hole in the side of the box as shown, leaving a margin of about 2" on all four sides.

2.   Cut two windows on both short sides of the box as shown, leaving a 2" margin on all the sides.

3.   Cut three 1" wide strips of cardboard. One strip should be the same length as the front of the box, and the other two the same width as the sides (see diagram). These strips will be used to strengthen the stage.

4.   To make the stage, cut strips of balsa wood: ½" × ½" × the length of the stage. Glue the strips to the bottom of the box, placing them in parallel lines exactly ½" apart (see diagram); continue until the entire bottom of the box is covered in this manner. The space between the strips of wood will be used to fit the wood stands of the characters as shown in the illustration. The characters can be moved on the stage by sliding them between the squares making the stage.

50

5. Paint the outside of the box a bright color with poster paints. Use another color for the inside of the box. With the illustration as a guide you can decorate your stage.

6. The stage curtain is made by cutting a piece of fabric to the size of the front of the box, with an inch added across the top. This extra inch is now folded over and glued down along the rough edge. When the glue has dried, cut the curtain in half. Now slide the string through . Secure each end of the string to the sides of the stage with staples. Now you can open and close the curtain during the performance. Be sure to choose a lightweight fabric for the curtain so that it hangs nicely.

On with the play!

Christmas Cards

Everyone loves to send and to receive Christmas cards. Christmas cards, which first appeared in the 1840s, are a good way of keeping in touch with friends and loved ones.

The star chosen for the design of one of our Christmas cards is an important symbol of Christmas. In ancient times people believed stars had magical powers. The brilliant star has always been a symbol of good luck. Wishes are made on the first star to come out at night. Sailors relied on the stars to guide them before they had compasses. It is said that a bright star rose high into the sky over the stable where the baby Jesus was born. The three Wise Men were guided by this star, the Star of Bethlehem.

The other Christmas card is of Santa Claus, our most famous gift-giver. Santa Claus has taken many forms and was not always a jolly old man dressed in a bright red suit. Our present idea of Santa Claus's appearance comes from Dr. Clement Moore's *A Visit from St. Nicholas*, the famous poem first published in a New York newspaper in 1823. But whether he's called Father Christmas, St. Nicholas, or Santa Claus, he's part of the desire to show love and goodwill at Christmastime.

Potato Print a Perfect Star

Here's a quick way to print a perfect star as many times as you like. One star can be printed on a small piece of paper that is folded over to make a message card. Four stars printed in different colors makes a beautiful Christmas card. You can cover a large piece of brown paper, a piece of newspaper, or shelving paper with many printed stars and create your own wrapping paper.

MATERIALS:

tracing paper
potato
paper to print on

poster paints or food coloring
knife
shallow dish
pencil, pins

METHOD:

1. Draw the pattern of the star on tracing paper and cut it out.

2. Cut a potato in half. Pin the pattern onto the flattest part of the potato half, using several pins.

3. Trace around the pattern with the point of the knife. Do not cut too deeply—just make a line.

4. Remove the pattern from the potato and cut out the area outside the star until the star design stands out ¼".

5. Cut a piece of paper and fold it to the size you want your finished card to be.

6. Put some paint into a shallow dish and dip the carved potato into it. Then press the potato firmly onto the paper. Watch out for dripping.

7. When you have lifted the potato from the paper you have your star design complete.

Repeat as many times as you like and change colors to vary the design. Experiment with overlapping the star points and printing one color on top of another. If you decide to print one star over another, let the first color dry first.

There are other designs for you to print. Follow the same steps as above after you have traced the patterns you want.

Ice-Skating Mr. and Mrs. Santa Claus Christmas Cards

This marvelous moving pair can be easily made. They can be sent as a special Christmas card. You can send both, or make up just one. Your friends can hang them on the Christmas tree. They will be a reminder of your good wishes— and cleverness.

MATERIALS:

white oaktag or lightweight cardboard
paper fasteners, pin
string or colored thread

pencil, cotton
scissors
tracing paper
business size envelope
felt tip markers

METHOD:

1.   Trace the pattern on the tracing paper and then transfer it onto the white oaktag.

2.   Cut the oaktag along the pattern lines.

3.   Draw in the details of the face, clothes, and skates with a felt tip marker. Then finish coloring.

4.   Glue the cotton onto the trim of the hat and clothes.

5.   Join the parts of the body with the paper fasteners as shown.

6.   Make a hole in the top with a pin, and attach a string or thread for hanging.

7.   In the center of the back there is enough space for your greeting. Use a felt tip marker.

8.   Put your card into a business size envelope and send it to a friend. Decorate the envelope a little with a pretty border or some printed stars.

58

Write a Christmas Greeting in Different Languages

Here's how to say "Merry Christmas" in many different ways from around the world. The words can also be made into interesting patterns.

BELGIUM—Zalig Kerstfeest
CHINA—Sheng Tan Kuai Loh
DENMARK—Glaedelig Jul
ENGLAND—Happy Christmas
FINLAND—Hauskaa Joulua
FRANCE—Joyeux Noel
GERMANY—Froehliche Weihnachten
GREECE—Eftihismena Christoughenna
IRELAND—Nodlaig mhaith chugnat
ITALY—Buon Natale

MEXICO—Feliz Navidad
NETHERLANDS—Hartelijke Kerstgroeten
NORWAY—Gledelig Jul
POLAND—Boze Narodzenie
PORTUGAL—Boas Festas
RUMANIA—Sarbatori Vesele
RUSSIA—Hristos Razdajetsja
SPAIN—Felices Pascuas
SWEDEN—Gud Jul
WALES—Nadolig Llawen

MATERIALS:

white paper
felt tip markers

METHOD:

1.   Take a piece of paper twice the size that you want your Christmas card to be, and fold it in half.

2.   You can use all these different ways of saying Merry Christmas and write them in many ways—in a circle that radiates from the center, around a square, or in a solid block. You can use just one language and repeat the same words one above the other. Or write each letter in a different color, or wide and thin. If you choose to use different languages, you can use different colors and sizes, too.

You can make this card using the traditional colors of Christmas, lively red, bright green, snowy white, and gleaming gold. Red stands for warmth and can be found on Santa's suit, holly berries, Christmas stockings and poinsettia plants. Green stands for natural things and can be found in the Christmas tree and wreaths. White stands for joy and purity and can be found in the mounds of Christmas snow. Gold stands for the sun's brilliance, the candle's glow and the shiny lights in shop windows.

Christmas Around the World

ENGLAND

English children hang up stockings the way we do in the hope that Father Christmas will fill them with treats. They write a letter to Father Christmas and then burn it in the fireplace. If the ashes go up the chimney, they'll get what they asked for. Children help their mothers prepare plum pudding and everyone has a turn stirring the batter and making a wish. A silver coin is put into the pudding before it is put into the oven to bake. Whoever finds the coin in their slice of pudding will have good luck for the new year.

IRELAND

On Christmas Eve throughout Ireland, the father places a candle in the front window and the youngest child lights it. This custom dates back to when the candle was a signal to the local priest that the family wanted him to say Christmas Mass in their home.

SYRIA

Syrian Christians also place a light in the window on Christmas Eve, to light the way for the Christ Child. A very tall candle is used so that it will burn all night.

PUERTO RICO

At the beginning of the Christmas season in Puerto Rico, small bands of carolers known as *trullas* make the rounds of friends and neighbors serenading them with traditional songs and often receiving gifts of money. The trullas usually travel on horseback in the rural areas, and as they go from farm to farm their numbers increase.

GERMANY

Most of our Christmas traditions began in Germany. One of the special events is a community Christmas tree lighting ceremony called the Bescherung. Sometimes real candles held in tiny tin dishes are attached to the tree and lighted.

MEXICO

In Mexico, people walk in a procession called La Posada to re-enact Mary and Joseph's search for shelter on the first Christmas. After this ceremony, children gather to strike open a piñata, a papier maché figure. This is usually in the shape of an animal like a bull, that is hung from the ceiling. All the children are blindfolded and given three chances to break the piñata with their stick. Inside the piñata are toys and candy which come showering down.

ITALY

The twelfth day after Christmas, January 6, is Epiphany, which commemorates the coming of the three Wise Men to the Christ Child in Bethlehem. This feast is celebrated in different ways in different countries. In Italy, La Befania, the merry witch, comes down the chimney and fills the stockings of good boys and girls with gifts. The bad children used to have coal put into their stockings, but today rock candy is used.

SWITZERLAND

Young people in Switzerland on their way to Midnight Mass on Christmas Eve stop at the Nine Fountains. At each fountain they take three sips of water. Legend says that those who do this will find their future love waiting at the door of the church.

FRANCE

In the French countryside the family celebrates when the Christmas log is brought into the house. The father lights the log after it has been sprinkled with wine.

AUSTRALIA

Australians usually go picnicking on Christmas Day because it's the middle of the summer there. But Santa Claus still wears a red woollen suit and the Christmas trees are full of artificial snow.

SPAIN

Spanish people dance in the streets after Midnight Mass, doing the special Christmas dance called La Jota.

NORWAY

Church bells ring all over Norway at 4 o'clock in the afternoon on Christmas Eve. This is a special custom which welcomes Christmas each year and is called *Ringe in Julen*.

POLAND

People bake *oplatki*, small wafers that are blessed and stamped with figures of the Nativity. These wafers are exchanged like Christmas cards.

NETHERLANDS

In the Netherlands—Holland—the Christmas season starts at the beginning of December with the birthday celebration for St. Nicholas, the children's saint. The Dutch children call him

Sinterklaas. He travels from where he lives in Spain to the Netherlands for the festivities. Church bells ring, everyone cheers and St. Nicholas parades through the city on his horse, a helper named *Peter* by his side.

The children put their wooden shoes or *sabots* in front of the fireplace before going to bed for St. Nicholas to fill with presents—or coal. School starts an hour later this morning to allow the children to enjoy the celebration.

PHILIPPINES

Children in the Philippines, where the weather is sunny and warm, make colorful Christmas wreaths and chains out of tropical flowers. After Christmas Mass, there is a great parade and everyone wears a wreath and carries a lighted candle.

DENMARK

An elf called *Jule Nissen* brings presents to the children of Denmark. The only one to see Jule Nissen is the family cat or perhaps a mischievous mouse. Everyone leaves a nice warm bowl of rice pudding for Jule Nissen to eat because he has such a long and hard journey delivering presents.

YUGOSLAVIA

Mothers in Yugoslavia bake a wonderful white Christmas cake filled with jelly candies. Like the English plum pudding the cake has a silver coin hidden inside. Whoever finds the coin in their piece of cake will have good luck.

SWEDEN

December 13 is Lucia Day in Sweden. A festival of lights, Lucia Day brightens the long dark Northern winter.

On this morning the oldest daughter of the family dresses in a white gown with a red sash. She plays Lucia, the Queen of Lights. She wears a beautiful crown of evergreens decked with lighted candles. Lucia brings a tray of coffee and special holiday treats called "Lucia cats" to her parents. "Lucia cats" are twisted saffron buns that have raisins for eyes.

Other people celebrate festivals of lights in the darkness of winter.

INDIA

Divali is the Hindu Festival of Lights. Before the holiday begins everyone makes clay lamps to be filled with oil. Wreaths are hung on the front doors of the houses and good luck designs are drawn with colored powders. Curry and special sweets are eaten. The walls and floors are white-washed and everyone wears new clothes. Gifts are exchanged and there are firework displays. As the sun goes down, the family strings the clay lamps along the roof, in the windows, and along the roads. Everywhere there are lights. These lights will guide Lakshmi, the Hindu goddess of good fortune, back to earth.

HANUKKAH, THE JEWISH FESTIVAL OF LIGHTS

This festival is celebrated in December by Jewish families around the world. Two thousand years ago, a small group of Israelites recaptured Jerusalem from the powerful foreign army that held it. The Israelites reclaimed their Holy Temple and rededicated it to God. There was only enough oil to keep the great candles on the eight-branched candleholder or Menorah burning for one day but a miracle kept the Menorah burning for eight days.

Hanukkah is celebrated for eight days, and gifts are exchanged each day. On the first night of Hanukkah one candle is lit in the Menorah. Each night one more candle is added until on the last night all eight candles are glowing.

Index